Book Description

Is she being over the top about everything lately? Does she give you a hard time with her dressing, food choices, and messy habits? Does she seem to have a mind of her own and disobey you on purpose?

Dear parents,

Welcome to the most dramatic and tough phase of your life.

Raising a teenage daughter is both hard and challenging. However, the right social skill set and parenting techniques can make it less daunting, and in some cases, even wonderful and rewarding.

Teaching our girls on how to communicate better, manage conflicts with their friends efficiently, act like responsible and disciplined adults, regulate their emotional fluctuations well, and remain transparent, and empathetic are all essential skills she needs to learn from you.

Thus, to help you start on the right foot, this book lists the 7 most effective parenting skills to not only understand your teenage daughter well but also be able to communicate with her and form a strong bond.

Written in a rather simple and easy-to-read and follow manner, hopefully, this will serve as a stress reliever for many parents struggling with raising a successful, happy, and confident teenager. It discusses the various changes that happen during adolescence as well as lists strategies on how to cope with them.

7 Vital Skills for Parenting Teen Girls and Communicating with Your Teenage Daughter

Proven Parenting Tips for Raising Teenage Girls with Self-Confidence and Coping Skills

Frank Dixon

professional advice. The content within this book has been derived from various sources. Please consult a licensed professional before attempting any techniques outlined in this book.

.

OTHER BOOKS BY FRANK DIXON

**How Parents Can Raise Resilient Children:
Preparing Your Child for the Real Tough World of
Adulthood by Instilling Them With Principles of
Love, Self-Discipline, and Independent Thinking**

❈ ❈ ❈

**How Parents Can Teach Children To Counter
Negative Thoughts: Channelling Your Child's
Negativity, Self-Doubt and Anxiety Into
Resilience, Willpower and Determination**

❈ ❈ ❈

**The Vital Parenting Skills and Happy Children
Box Set: A 5 Full-Length Parenting Book
Compilation for Raising Happy Kids Who Are
Honest, Respectful and Well-Adjusted**

❈ ❈ ❈

**The 7 Vital Parenting Skills and Confident Kids
Box Set: A 7 Full-Length Positive Parenting Book
Compilation for Raising Well-Adjusted Children**

❈ ❈ ❈

**For a complete list, please visit
http://bestparentingbooks.org/books**

YOUR FREE GIFT

Before we begin, I have something special waiting for you. Another action-paced book, free of cost. Think of it as my way of saying thank you to you for purchasing this.

Your gift is a special PDF actionable guide titled, ***"Profoundly Positive Parenting: Learn the Top 10 Skills to Raising Extraordinary Kids!"***

As the title suggests, it's a collection of 10 parenting skills that will help you pave the way towards raising amazing and successful children. It's short enough to read quickly, but meaty enough to offer actionable advice that can make impactful changes to the way you parent.

Intrigued, I knew you would be!

Claim your copy of Profoundly Positive Parenting by clicking on the link below and join my mailing list:

http://bestparentingbooks.org/free-gift/

PROFOUNDLY

POSITIVE PARENTING

Learn the Top 10 Parenting Skills
to Raising Extraordinary Kids!

FRANK DIXON

Before we jump in, I'd like to express my gratitude. I know this mustn't be the first book you came across and yet you still decided to give it a read. There are numerous courses and guides you could have picked instead that promise to make you an ideal and well-rounded parent while raising your children to be the best they can be.

But for some reason, mine stood out from the rest and this makes me the happiest person on the planet right now. If you stick with it, I promise this will be a worthwhile read.

In the pages that follow, you're going to learn the best parenting skills so that your child can grow to become the best version of themselves and in doing so experience a meaningful understanding of what it means to be an effective parent.

Notable Quotes About Parenting

"Children Must Be Taught How To Think, Not What To Think."

— Margaret Mead

"It's easier to build strong children than to fix broken men [or women]."

- Frederick Douglass

"Truly great friends are hard to find, difficult to leave, and impossible to forget."

— George Randolf

"Nothing in life is to be feared, it is only to be understood. Now is the time to understand more, so that we may fear less."

— Scientist Marie Curie

Table of Contents

Introduction

"But, mom, you don't know anything..."

One of the most common cries of a teenage daughter. Teenagers, in general, are rebellious creatures. They are also unpredictable and secretive. They will close the door on your face when talking to someone on their phones, lie to you about going to a sleepover at a friend while packing their most provocative dress in their bags. However, they aren't all bad. In fact, as they grow older and steer their way towards entering adulthood, they become the best of friends. A bond between a teenage daughter and a mother or a father and his son is often spoken of. For parents, it is one of the most challenging yet delightful periods of their lives because they finally get to see them grow into these beautiful birds ready to leave the nest in some time.

That growth doesn't come without challenges. In fact, many parents think that living with a teenager is like living with a stranger in the house. The lines of communication are mostly jammed and there is no way to know what they are thinking or doing or thinking to do. If you are a parent with a teenager in the house, you will get the joke.

Since we are going to focus on teenage daughters, the dramas, the self-esteem, and body image issues here, let's try to visualize what daily life with a teenage daughter looks like.

For starters, teenage daughters believe that the parents are the straight-up target for releasing all the pent-up frustration and anger. You will often find yourself being labeled as unconcerned, uncompassionate, and naïve. However, to blame them for all the chaos in the house will be one side of the story. Unlike old times, our daughters don't have it easy today. They have to deal with tons of stressors which lead to unwanted anxiety and depression. They are subjected to bullying for looking a certain way and develop eating disorders because of it. They are also exposed to things like substance abuse, sexual experimentation, harassment, and whatnot. Things weren't always the same before. Friendships nurtured during sleepovers when pals went ghost-hunting. There were fewer secrets and each presented the other with an honest opinion. There was less judgment and more compassion.

It is ironic that although we have more resources than ever to teach girls to cope with the stressors, their life seems too pressure-optimized. On the other hand, this leaves parents to deal with excessive worry and feel incompetent to help them in some way.

As a parent, you might often ask yourself how to help them feel safe and confident, how to make them feel more in control of their lives, how to teach them to carry the world on their backs fearlessly and the answer is simple: you teach them some basic coping, communication, and relationship management skills. When you teach them these, you make this testing phase of their lives easier to pass through.

In this book, we shall look at 7 essential skills to teach teenage daughters to make their lives stress-free and manageable. It will also benefit you to build a deeper and stronger bond with them and become an important part of their lives and experiences. The stronger the bond, the stronger the communication. The stronger the communication, the fewer the secrets. The fewer the secrets, the more the trust between you two. So, you see, it is like a chain that ends with a fulfilling and harmonious experience for the two of you.

So, without further delay, let's begin.

Chapter 1: The Growing Teenager

You can be certain about one thing: Today's teenagers are stronger and more spirited than ever. They will stand up against what's wrong and won't back down when it comes to having their opinions heard. They are generally more empathetic and smarter than previous generations, too. They will have a say about anything and everything and feel things more deeply. The reason can be contributed to their exposure to the world via the internet and social media. It should surely be counted as a blessing, but we also know of its dark side and how harmful it can be for a young adult to cope with the pressures of it.

Most of the time, these changes not only affect them on the whole but also the parents. It leaves you confused about how to respond and react to the situations you find yourself in and no matter how many parenting books or articles you have read online, the reality is too real and difficult to handle. As they try to be more in control and independent, there is sometimes a clash between you two. You are then expected to have a cool head and manage and prevent conflicts before they escalate and you two drift apart.

In this first chapter, we look at the various social, physical, and emotional changes they go through and how they affect their behavior, attitude, and mood. The changes are mostly puberty-related, which means they can't be blamed for all the chaos they create because they are a part of it, too. If it is hard being a parent, it is also hard to be a teenager and go through so many transitions at once without having proper knowledge of it.

Physical, Emotional and Social Changes

During adolescence, it is common to notice many cognitive, social, and emotional changes in young girls. The way their interactions change, the way they form friendships, the way they search for their identities are all aspects of the many changes happening within them. Physical changes being the easiest to decipher and note. However, many emotional and social changes also occur that we must take into account trying to learn about their mood, behavior, and interactions.

Physical Changes

Puberty can start as early as eight or as late as about thirteen. The standard, however, is set at about 10 years of age. Puberty is what leads to the many bodily changes we see in teenage girls. Some of the most common changes in their physical appearance include:

- Breast Development: Breast development or budding is one of the most prominent indicators of puberty. Girls develop nickel-sized bumps under their nipples and their nipples become sore and tender.

- Body Hair: Girls, when they hit puberty notice coarse growth of hair in their underarms, legs, and around the genital area. Pubic hair, according to many, is the first indicator of puberty.
- Periods: Periods is the most important indicator of reaching puberty. The timelines can vary but if we talk about the USA, the average age for a girl to have her first period is about 12 years.
- Increase in Height: Unlike boys, girls have a faster growth spurt and begins before their first period. The earliest signs of height growth are when their breasts start to bud, around six to eight months before their first period. It must also be noted that by the time a girl has her first period, the rate of their height growth decreases, and they only grow one or two inches taller after that.
- Wider Hips: Girls also notice their waist becoming smaller and their hips becoming wider.
- Sweating and Body Odor: Sweating under the armpits is another common occurrence when girls are turning into women. They may need to shower more often and apply deodorant in their armpits to avoid smelling bad.

Emotional Changes

Now that she is turning into a beautiful young adult, you may notice the show of strong feelings and intense emotions. Their mood becomes unpredictable and they demonstrate many ups and downs at varying times which makes it harder for parents to interpret and respond accordingly. Thus, the increase in the number of conflicts at home because they feel unheard, misunderstood, and unvalued. Most of the blame can be put on the different chemicals in their brain and their lack of emotional intelligence. They are unable to process and express their emotions like grown-ups and it leads to an increased amount of frustration. Some other significant emotional changes include:

- Increased Sensitivity: With time, they become better at processing other's emotions which in turn, makes them empathetic. However, they may still have a difficult time reading or decode facial expressions and body language.
- Become Self-conscious: Suddenly, the way they look is all that matters. They become conscious about the many physical changes they are going through and it affects their self-esteem. With little knowledge about their unique stature, they start to compare themselves with other girls in their school and feel insecure.
- Lack of Decision-making skills: many teenage girls think that they are invincible. They think that they are queens of the kingdom and thus

want to rule. However, this often leads to bad decision-making such as dating the wrong boy or using unhealthy and damaging products for their skin, face, and hips without the knowledge of their parents, to become more desirable.

Social Changes

Young girls are so worried about where they fit into this world that they are always searching to associate themselves with someone or something. This is the age when they begin to idolize their teachers, celebrities, social influencers, or their parents. They try to put themselves into a certain box. Either they are hot or they aren't. Either they are thin and skinny or fat. Either they are popular or unpopular etc. they will put on different clothes, get their hair dyed after crying for a week in front of their parents or start dieting. As parents, you must know that this is just a normal phase in their lives. They are just trying to figure out their standing. With time, their sense of identity becomes stronger and they get a better sense of who they want to be like when they grow up. Other than that, you can expect them to depict the following changes.

- Seek Independence: their need for independence increases. They want to decide for themselves or at least have a say in matters concerning them.
- Develop a Sense of Morals: They will start to differentiate between right and wrong. They

will start to take responsibility for their actions and be ready to suffer the consequences of a bad decision. They will also be inquisitive about the right morals and values.

- Seek More Responsibility: They will start to own up to their actions, both at home and in school, and be more willing to work on their strengths and weaknesses.
- Seek New Experiences: As they learn to gain control of their impulses, you can expect them to indulge in some risky behaviors such as self-harm over a heartbreak or driving while intoxicated. This is the doing of their brains that encourages them to try new things and seek more out-of-the-world experiences.
- Become Influenced Easily: They also seem to be easily influenced by their peers, role models, and other influencers they follow on their social media accounts. They will try to be like them, do what they do, or just be inspired to grow up to be like them one day. Most girls this age, fantasize about TV celebrities, movie stars, and the "bad boys" in their school, and have imaginary romantic relationships with them.
- Explore Sexual Identify: Talking of romance, the hormonal balances, and the puberty-related changes also make them want to try sexual things with a partner. Most teenagers do it out of curiosity or because others are doing it, too. They may also have intimate

relationships early one which is why it is highly critical that you discuss with them the topic of safe sex in detail. You must also tell them that they shouldn't feel pressured to do anything they don't want to do and report to you if anyone forces them, too.

Mood Swings, Social Media, and Independence

As stated, puberty brings along a new set of challenges and changes. The physical changes young girls go through during the first three to four years can trigger many body-image related issues. The less confident they are, the poorer their self-esteem. Hence, you can expect them to be always a little self-conscious about what they are wearing especially during the days of menstruation or looking like with pimples and acne breakouts on their face. The onset of the discomfort can have a significant impact on their mood. They may seem anxious, angry, or depressed.

Moreover, their brain is still in the process of developing with the prefrontal cortex as its main candidate. This region of the brain is responsible for decision-making and judgment, which is why we may notice some poor decision-making on their part about their choices and preferences. However, since it is just a phase, their choices change with time, and their capacity to make sensible decisions improves, too.

Mood Swings and Teen Girls

We have often seen a stereotypical image of a difficult daughter in movies and TV shows where the parents feel helpless when it comes to knowing how to handle them. They can be seen fighting with their siblings over insignificant things like a TV's remote or sitting in the front seat of the car when driving to school. A lot of times, this anger is a way of releasing the pressure and frustration they feel within.

According to one study, teenage daughters do suffer from mood swings when they are growing (Maciejewski et al., 2015). Some 500 adolescents were called in for experimentation. Their ages ranged from 13 to 18. The teenage girls were told to keep an online account of their daily happiness, sadness, anger, and anxiety for the next five days. After reviewing the individual responses, the researchers found that mood swings were quite prevalent in early adolescence. The girls showed extreme variations in their level of happiness and sadness.

For a parent, it can be hard to deal with the ups and downs they go through. They are unable to know what to do and can be quite confused. Therefore, to make sense of the situations, they label them as disrespectful or difficult which isn't the case.

Social Media, Body Image, and Teen Girls

Body-image is a critical issue with young girls. As they start to sprout, they become extremely concerned about the way they look and feel. They become insecure about their looks and the pressure to look good and healthy on social media just adds to that pressure.

During an interesting online survey by Common Sense Media, 35% of the teenagers (girls) are worried about being tagged in unattractive photos and videos by their friends without their consent. Another 27% of them feel stressed whenever posting a picture of themselves on their social accounts, uncertain about how it will be received. Further, 22% of them feel extremely sad and worried when they don't receive any likes or comments on them (Rideout & Robb, 2019).

On one hand, social media helps us to stay connected and be aware of everything happening around the world and on the other, it is raising a generation of self-conscious young men and women who go to extreme lengths to look 'beautiful' According to one study, the use of Facebook is linked to an increased risk of eating disorders among young girls (Mabe et al., 2014).

Not to mention, social media also gives rise to incidents of cyberbullying (Anderson, 2018). Some people feel bad because they are mocked for being different while others feel left out and unnoticed. It is wise to say that the cons outweigh the cons when it comes to one's mental health and peace of mind. During a TV show called #Being Thirteen: Inside the Secret World of Teens, a group of thirteen-year-olds was called in for a survey. The researchers found that those who spent/checked in on social media 50 to 100 times a day were less happy and satisfied with their lives than those who checked it only a few times per day.

Independence and Teen Girls

The growing need for independence is another sign of adolescent development. Teen girls become more responsible, figure out their values and morals, and express themselves through their fashion choices, friends, the music they listen to, or hobbies they are interested in. they may not always be in line with the ones made by their parents and thus, conflicts may arise.

They want to be able to make decisions for themselves. However, they aren't always the right decisions and you might want to save them from the hurt and damage early on. However, because it isn't coming from them, they might not take those opinions too well. Again, no need to worry as failure is the best teacher. The more times they fail, the more valuable lessons they learn. This also helps them develop resilience i.e. coming out of a bad experience with their head held high. For you, it mustn't be easy to know that they are going to fall and still not lend a hand. Don't! Or else, they may see it as a conflicting opinion and deliberately attempt that thing just to prove you wrong.

Chapter 2: A Parent's Essential Toolkit

Many parents believe that raising a teenager is a nightmare. There is so much you want to do for them but they don't let you. They choose their paths, fight to get their way, make friends you don't approve of, keep secrets, and go behind your back on several occasions, and whatnot. This can take a toll on the parents as there is nothing that prepares them for this kind of attitude. Although not all kids behave this badly, it can be said for most of them. They find their parents a little old-fashioned. The last time they checked, you had scolded them over a joke they cracked and given them a full 10 minutes lecture over it. So, you can understand their hesitance to come to you with their problems. Also, in many homes, the relationship between a parent and a daughter is more dictatorial and less friendly. So, what to do and what not to do, can be rather tricky. Thus, to get you started on the right foot, here are seven essential skills to teach them right from the start.

A Guide to the 7 Essential Parenting Skills to Teach Teenage Daughters

Isn't it odd that your once lovely, smiley little one is fuming with anger, hiding things from you, and doing things their way just to push your buttons?

Whatever suggestions you make are wrong and everything you do or say is old-fashioned.

As children grow older, parents need to adopt new parenting techniques. Yesterday, they needed to be shown how to eat, chomp on their food, go potty, and dress but today, they need to be told how to behave, resolve conflicts, express themselves, be transparent and listen. You may think that they no longer need a parent-figure in their lives now that they act all grown-up. You are mistaken. They need you more than ever to teach them some essential skills to make this phase of their lives easier. They need you to guide and mentor them by instilling good habits as well as teaching them some basic communication, coping and conflict resolution skills to feel confident in their skins and have high self-esteem. You need to implement strategies that will enable them to own up to their mistakes, stay disciplined, and not give in to the pressures of social media and cyberbullying.

Thus coming to the 7 essential skills this book is all about, take a look at the skills we think to cut and are deemed most valuable to teach.

Essential Parenting Skill #1: Communication and Listening Skills

She needs to learn to talk. Period. She must know how to make herself heard, listen without judgment, and express herself in a disciplined and consistent manner. Good communication skills from an early age also make children more empathetic and compassionate towards others and their feelings. She must also learn to carry herself respectfully in social gatherings, and with people of different ages, manage negative emotions, and prevent arguments from turning into bigger disagreements. Therefore, as a parent, be concerned if she isn't picking up these skills as these are what sets the foundation for the rest.

Essential Parenting Skill #2: Values, Discipline, and Responsibilities

All teenagers must know what is expected of them. They must know to adhere to the rules set by their parents and teachers and avoid misbehaving. Teaching them how to be responsible, own up to their shortcomings, and be disciplined is a parent's job. Again, these are things whose foundations you have to lay early on as most children when they hit their tweens and teen years begin to demonstrate a lack of empathy and discipline. They start to take others for granted, including their parents, and make it harder for those parents to parent.

Essential Parenting Skill #3: Conflict Resolution and Management

Conflicts arise when there is a disagreement of some sort between people. They can be minor and resolved with both the parties sitting together and sorting it out or major where adults have to intervene. Teenage daughters face tens of conflicts, if not more, daily. Conflicts can be highly stressful for her and can lead to depression and panic attacks. Many teens don't do well with it, and thus, as parents, we have to teach them how to cope with the emotions that arise as a result and healthily deal with them.

Essential Parenting Skill #4: Combat Body-Image Issues and Cyberbullying

With the advancement of technology, social media addiction is becoming a real and scary thing. Children, especially teenagers spend more time online than they should, exposing themselves to all sorts of heinous, obscene, and self-destructive things. Social media has also given rise to cyberbullying, in which many teenage girls become the victim. They are laughed at, mocked, and made fun of online by their classmates and friends all the time which can lead to some serious self-esteem issues in them. Therefore, as a parent, it is your job to limit the amount of time she spends browsing the internet and control the type of content she exposes herself, too. This accounts for setting some ground rules that you must teach her about as well as how to cope with the pressures that come with it.

Essential Parenting Skill #5: Empathy, Compassion, and Emotional Intelligence

With her ego taking over her life, she hardly shows an ounce of compassion and empathy. She also has a troubled time dealing with the many new emotions and feelings they go through. Therefore, she must be taught how to manage the onset of difficult emotions, behave, and act well-mannered and show compassion towards others.

Essential Parenting Skill #6: Honesty and Transparency

Honesty and transparency mean that no lies are told and no secrets are kept. As our girls start their journey towards becoming a woman, they encounter many challenges. They become distant from their parents and they form more intimate bonds with their partners and friends. They start to slam doors in the face, yell, and roll their eyes. However, this shouldn't stop parents from teaching them to remain honest and transparent. They must feel comfortable sharing stuff with you and express themselves without feeling judged.

Essential Parenting Skill #7: Relationship Management

Relationship management refers to the art of maintaining and supervising different relationships one forms with another. It entails the building of strong interpersonal communication skills as well as the ability to form bonds that help you and your partner nurture, grow, develop, and resolve conflicts. Since young girls start to look up to others and form bonds with their peers, it is important to teach them how to maintain strong friendships and learn to resolve any conflicts that arise.

Chapter 3: Essential Parenting Skill – Communication

Communication is one of the most essential life skills. Humans have used it as a means to express themselves, have their needs fulfilled, and form bonds. If we think about it, we have been communicating from the minute we were born. First, we cried to demand food and a diaper change, then picked up a few words and then started to speak full sentences at the age of three or four. So, you might wonder, if we have been doing it for so long, why do we still need to learn it? Why do we need to teach our teenage sons and daughters to do it? It is because if we don't, we will not be able to pick up the meaning of what has been said. Ask yourself this, if you don't know the meaning of a specific word, how can you use it in a sentence? Similarly, if you don't understand what has been said to you, you can't form a proper response or reaction. You can't communicate back until you understand the context and meaning of it.

Therefore, it is an essential social skill all parents must teach their children so that they can be raised as knowledgeable, smart, and vigilant. They can read between the lines, i.e. pick up the context of something using non-verbal cues such as facial expressions, body language, physical action, the tone of voice, etc.

Importance of Building Effective Communication skills in Teenage Daughters

Everything we say or do sends a message. We may not even realize but our body language may communicate on behalf of us. Such as, if we are sitting through a three-hour workshop session, we may not even realize we are sleepy until we have yawned at least twice. If we are caught, what does that say about us or the speaker? This means that it is easy to form judgments even when one isn't actively communicating.

Good communication skills are like that icing on the cake that makes it all the more delicious and tempting. It allows us an upper hand over the receiver. The more sound and sensible we are, the easier it is for the receiver to understand and form an opinion.

For teenagers, effective communication skills allow them to be perceived well. It adds an element of awareness and confidence. When they depict good communication skills, it makes the message more meaningful. Moreover, it allows them to be as expressive or impassive as they want to be. When teenagers can hold conversations with others, it also boosts their confidence and self-esteem. It allows them to speak their minds which helps them cultivate meaningful relationships with everyone.

Teaching Her to Listen, Talk, and Connect

Since the book is about encouraging communication in young girls, we must know that most of them look up to their moms for guidance and mentorship. From an early age, they have been imitating your actions, behaviors, and moods. Remember the time they would want to dress up like you, wear your shoes, and apply your makeup... Since they look up to us as their role models, it is time we become one. The point being: if you want to teach her effective communication skills, you have to model it yourself. How you resolve conflicts, hold communication, express yourself, demonstrate happiness or anger are all ways that she is going to pick up.

Therefore, to emphasize the importance of learning how to communicate, you have to be her teacher. You have to be smart about it, too. Because chances are, if you come onto her as if giving her a lecture or ordering her, she is going to misbehave and disobey. You have to act and think like a teenager and mold your words in such a manner that it reaches her head as well as her hearts. So, what else can you do to help her learn how to communicate? Take a look below!

Spend Time With Her

The most effective strategy to boost their confidence in their ability to converse well is by providing them the opportunities to do so. Seek their opinion over things, ask them about their day, discuss the days' activities, talk to them about their friends, read, eat, and watch TV together.

Praise Her

Constant nagging creates distance. You don't want that. You want her to come to you with all her problems no matter how naïve or complicated they are. They will likely roll their eyes or slam the door on you if you are a harsh critique and keep finding faults in her. On the other hand, if you use praise, appreciation, and recognition to your advantage, you might get through to her. She might open up to you when she notices that you don't judge her choices, values her opinions, and praises her for the good she does.

Use Social Media to Your Advantage

If you feel you are incapable to find something interesting to talk about, you can always use social media as a tool to help you bond. If you are friends with her on Facebook or Instagram, you must be able to view the type of content that interests her. Take a look at what she likes and comments on. You can always talk about it with her over dinner or during her free time to encourage communication.

Be the Parent

Although you might want to give her some space and privacy, this shouldn't mean that she can get away with whatever she likes. You have to lay some basic ground rules such as when she is and isn't allowed to close her door, until what time she can stay out with her friends, who can/can't be invited over, etc. Having these in place will prevent conflicts later. Also, it will make her grow up to be disciplined and value rules and regulations in the professional world.

Teach Her How to Express Herself

She must know how to express herself efficiently. This means she must know how to stay calm in panicking situations, use words instead of anger to articulate it, and practice good communication etiquette when speaking to an elder or a toddler, etc.

Enforce Effective Listening Skills

Teach her how to listen attentively without being distracted when talking to someone. An essential part of effective communication is good listening which involves devoting your complete attention to the speaker. When undivided attention is given to someone, it shows strong character and genuine concern. She must also know how to ask or probe questions in a polite manner when she isn't able to comprehend something.

Teach Her to Notice Body Language

Sometimes, you don't need words to express yourself. Your body language does it for you. However, teens may have difficulty picking up non-verbal cues and making wrong assumptions. Therefore, encourage the art of observation.

Additionally, make her notice her body language when she is in different states of mind such as happy, angry, sad, or distracted. You can make a video of her depicting any of these and then watch it together to put forward some suggestions on how to improve.

Get Together to Critique

If you want to teach her how to open up to you and others, one of the best ways to do is by getting on board with her to read or watch a book or film together and then critique it. You can also create a YouTube channel together and upload reaction videos where you share your thoughts about something you just reviewed. You can discuss the things you liked or disliked, things that could have been improved or taken out, etc. This encourages storytelling in kids, which again, is a great form of communication.

Encourage Blogging or Journaling

Journaling or simply keeping a diary has been proven therapeutic for teenagers. It allows them to vent out their emotions on a paper in a healthy and low-stress way. They can be who they are when they are writing a diary and express feelings they have kept bottled up. Encourage your teenage daughter to keep a diary and record day-to-day events in it. If she isn't old-school, you may also suggest turning to the internet and starting a blog. With the whole world online, she will surely find someone going through the same and be able to connect with her and improve her communication skills in the process.

Chapter 4: Essential Parenting Skill – Conflict Management

During the teen ages, we have more clashes with our kids than we ever had in the past. For instance, when they were young, they would mostly wear things you made them wear but now they might have a difference of opinion. They may want to pick their dresses and wear something you don't approve of. You may also have differences of opinions on whether they should own a car or not before they turn eighteen, whether they should have sleepovers or not etc.

These types of conflicts are healthy and normal as it tells us about each other's expectations. You understand her need for independence and she understands your need regarding her safety. However, sometimes, conflicts can turn nasty. They may become so big that all channels of communication between the two of you get blocked.

Thus, you both need to know of some good conflict management and resolution strategies to deal with them, resolve them, and then move on. When you and your children are on the same boat, aka living in harmony, it reduces the family's stress levels. It can also result in a healthy and strong relationship with your child. Knowing how to deal with conflicts effectively is yet another essential skill to teach your teenage daughter. With her hormones raging and mood swings taking over her better judgment, she will be making many enemies, too. She will probably go through heartbreaks, end ties with lifelong friends, and deal with the pressure-inducing demands from her school. Equipping her with the right skills to deal with all of these things can be rewarding shortly when she graduates and enters the professional world.

Importance of Teaching Conflict Management Skills

All-day long, she confronts conflicts when she has a disagreement with you over something, with her best friend about not replying to her texts sooner, or with her boyfriend who seems more interested in playing ball with his friends than talking to her. It is almost impossible to protect them from conflicts and thus, they must know how to deal with them respectively.

After all, she can't avoid people all her life. She must know how to make confrontations less scary. She must know how to deal with a differentiating opinion and hear what others have to say. Learning to deal with conflicts allows us to get along with others better. We feel more control of the situation when we successfully handle any issue that may have led to becoming a conflict.

Therefore, you must teach your daughter how to manage them.

Teaching Our Girls to Resolve Conflicts

For centuries, women have been expected to be the paragons of inclusivity and acceptance. They have been told to be like Mother Teresa, selfless, and forgiving. They have been told to model acceptance and embrace compassion. This school of thought has done some drastic damage to the making of a woman who views these values important and chooses to remain in unhealthy and toxic relationships. This has to stop. We mustn't raise our teenage daughters to such injustice. We need to set better values and instill better and empowering skills in them to not bend at the face of a conflict but rise and hold a sword. We have to read with them stories about women who became the heroes of their own stories instead of telling them to rely on their counterparts for everything. We have to tell them that it is completely okay to not want to be friends with everyone.

We have to teach our girls to navigate through conflicts with confidence without bowing down their heads and taking the blame for everything.

So how can we, as parents, help them manage conflicts in a non-toxic and healthy manner? Let's learn below.

Plan in Advance

Teen girls tend to be impulsive. They rarely take the time out to think things rationally before speaking them out like venom on others. Chances are if she doesn't know what to say and when to say it, she will have many regrets to cry over, later. Therefore, encourage her to seek advice from someone older and wiser than her, such as you, when she finds herself in a conflicting situation. When she knows she can look up to someone for consultation, she will avoid being rude and unreasonable.

Don't Call in an Audience

Sometimes, teenagers believe that having an audience or support system behind them during a confrontation makes them appear stronger. True, but it can also escalate things further, when more secrets are out, feelings are hurt and emotions run high. Therefore, if she has a problem with someone, say a girl from her class, she must choose to talk to her directly in a one-on-one conversation. This will prevent the confrontation from becoming a fight scene from the Mean Girls.

Use 'I' Instead of 'You'

Using statements starting with 'I' are less conflicting. They are less provoking and yet direct. Statements starting with 'you,' on the other hand, blamed others. Take a look at what we mean by this:

- "I feel sad that you told everyone about that incident after school."
- "You are so mean. You told everyone about that incident after school."

Notice the difference in the tone and emotions in each of these sentences. The first one seems less disputable than the second one.

Admit Mistakes

Another important thing to teach your daughter is to admit when she is wrong and apologize. Doing so diffuses the situation instantly and prevents the escalation of the conflict. She must know what genuine apology sounds like and how to make the other person understand her situation without being loud, or angry. A good apology must list the amends she is going to make to dissolve the situation and prevent further conflict.

Breathe In and Breathe Out

Sometimes, while discussing a friend, she may get all riled up and fumed. Teach her some basic breathing skills to not lose her temper and stay calm. Breathing in and out for about a minute when she feels too overwhelmed with her emotions can help her relax and think rationally.

Calm Her Down

Just because they have broken up with a friend doesn't mean that friend automatically becomes an enemy. Your daughter should know that it is okay to move on and not hold onto a grudge forever. Easier said than done, teach her to let go and move on. Tell her that friendships end for a lot of reasons and it doesn't mean that they will never have a friend again or trust someone so deeply.

Chapter 5: Essential Parenting Skill – Coping with Body-Image Issues and Cyber Bullying

Did you know, kids form an opinion about their bodies from an early age, as little as three? It is the time when their tiny brains begin to understand the concept of thin and fat and also the age where they actively start to seek idols and role models. They want to look like them and when they don't, they feel disheartened. A lot of young girls who see ballerinas and models on TV want to be like them when they grow up and in their little mind, it all starts with looking petite.

Here, the role of the parents is a crucial one as they have to save them from succumbing to the ideals they think are normal when they aren't. It is our job to implant the right ideas about body image and self-esteem.

Although it is very difficult in this age and time to escape the idea promoted by social media and advertising companies, it is still imperative that we teach our young girls to not fall into the traps they lay. We must ensure that they take the right message from an ad they see and not just want to blindly follow others like a herd. Still, how much can you shield them from? She is going to school, on social media, and looking at hot girls dating the hot guys. It's simple math. So, whenever she looks at herself in the mirror, she sees all the flaws instead of the things that make her stand out. She focuses only on outward beauty and not what lies within because in her naïve mind, that is what matters. She thinks her body has to be perfect. She thinks having the perfect body will earn her acceptance, love, and admiration from others. She thinks it will make her happy.

The only problem is that there is no absolute definition of beauty. Not long ago, being petite and a size zero was considered the epitome of beauty but today's research reveals that men like to date women with curvy bodies. They admire rounder hips, a blossomed chest, and thick legs. So, chasing after something that may change tomorrow doesn't make sense, right? Besides, let's not even get started on how much editing and photoshopping goes into making models and celebrities look perfect on cover magazines.

Young girls want to look like them and when they don't their self-esteem suffers (Huebscher, 2010).

You can't let your daughter go through the same mental torture or allow her to be bullied online by her mates and friends. The damages done may be irreversible. Since it is harder to shut down the haters and move on with our lives, why don't we teach our girls to be happy in their skin? Why don't we teach her that she doesn't have to starve herself to lose weight and instead, have a healthy and balanced diet? Why don't we teach her that she has to accept and appreciate the beauty that she is and not try to compare herself with every single person she goes to school with?

Teaching Her to Own Her Uniqueness

We know, as their parents, the importance of nurturing a positive body image, however, it isn't us that we have to convince, it is our teenage daughters. We have to make them understand that to grow into healthy and well-rounded adults, they can't continue to starve their bodies and deprive it of the basic nutrients. We have to brainwash them about the idols they fixate on and introduce to them inspiring personalities like Oprah Winfrey, Michelle Obama, Hilary Clinton, Serena Williams, and more who are more than just pretty faces we see on our TV screens. These are the kind of powerful women your daughter should look up to. She must follow in their footsteps and aim to become great and inspirational, not just someone everyone calls pretty.

It is sad to see girls, who get the best grades in school and have terrific talents and yet, feel like they aren't good enough. So, what can we do to disregard such a mindset and encourage them to own their uniqueness?

Focus on Inner Beauty

The first thing you need to tell your daughter is to focus on being a good person instead of being a pretty person. It is one's character and personality that makes them likable, not their looks. Start by praising her for her positive attributes such as how calm she is all the time, how honest she is, how sincere she is towards her friends, how much she values her family's values and traditions etc. She needs to see that it is these things that make a person appear beautiful in the eyes of others and not their outer beauty.

Promote Healthy Eating Behaviors

Children take up most behaviors from their parents. If they see you snacking on unhealthy snacks all the time or eating at abrupt hours, she will pick up the same habit. Your job is to not normalize such behavior for her, but rather encourage good eating habits. Introduce to her a variety of fruits and vegetables to snack on when she feels hungry. Indulge in low-fat dairy products lean meats and processed cereals and, avoid processed meat, high in sugar content, and fizzy drinks. She can always snack on some junk food occasionally but don't allow too much of it.

Discourage Dieting

Never encourage your child to diet as it can lead to worrisome symptoms like low blood pressure, fatigue, nausea, weakness, constipation, dehydration, and headaches. Too much dieting can turn into an eating disorder like bulimia or anorexia. Besides, some studies prove that those who diet regain the lost weight in less time than what they spent dieting (Mann, 2018). Therefore, talk to her about the dangers of it and why she must never do it.

Avoid Negative Body Talk

When around her, don't point out her flaws. You are the last person she wants to be criticized by. This also goes for your own body. You have to feel confident in the way you look so that she picks up that, too. You must work on modeling a healthy acceptance and not complain about the ugly parts such as the sagginess of your skin, muffin top on your belly, or the loose skin on your thighs. Also, don't emphasize physical appearances. If she is suffering from low self-esteem due to it, you have to uplift it by talking about the different aspects of what makes her beautiful.

Exercise But Not to Lose Fat

There is a difference between exercising to stay healthy and exercising to lose weight. Make exercising a fun activity without focusing too much on the losing weight aspect of it. it is more important that she feels healthy than pretty. Plan events like hiking trips to the beach, or to the farmer's market where more walking is involved. You can even go to parks near your house for a jog or rent bikes to go cycling on the weekends.

Chapter 6: Essential Parenting Skill – Empathy

Have you ever noticed how your teenage daughter has no compassion for others? You give her some bad news about a relative's illness and she rarely nudges with discomfort or apology. Does it also have a hard time looking at things from a different person's perspective and always focusing on herself? Does she find herself struggling to engage in activities that only benefit others, say like volunteering?

She isn't trying to be mean on purpose, she just lacks the basic empathy skills, that's all!

For most parents, it is easier to just jump to the conclusion that their child isn't empathetic. They don't shed a tear when a butterfly they spent caring for after it injured one of its wings, dies after a week. They don't feel guilty when proving someone wrong. They don't feel ashamed when they don't give up their seat on the bus to a handicapped kid in their school. Although it does seem like they lack the caring nerve, it isn't true. Luckily, empathy can be nurtured at almost every age.

Your teenage daughter may also have some issues with emotional intelligence. You may have a difficult time trying to understand her or her odd behavior. According to one study, it isn't her fault, but her brain's fault.

The research suggests that the way a teenager's brain develops during adolescence may affect empathy (Graaff et al., 2014).

Most people master concrete thinking skills when they enter secondary school. However, our executive functioning skills like organization, planning, self-control, decision-making, and other such areas can take longer to establish themselves. Research suggests that our affective empathy and cognitive empathy skills also develop during the teen years. Affective empathy refers to the ability to recognize and respond to the feelings of others appropriately whereas cognitive empathy refers to the ability to see things from a different person's perspective and think mentally. Both of these skills hold importance in helping teenagers cope with the social pressures they face, manage their and others' emotions, and prevent conflict.

However, different regions of the brain are responsible for affective and cognitive empathy. Affective empathy relates to the limbic region whereas cognitive empathy is grounded in the medial prefrontal cortex of the brain. Since these two are linked, it shows that a child's affective empathy can be a predictor of the level of cognitive empathy as teenagers. In girls, affective empathy remains stable and relatively high throughout adolescence whereas cognitive empathy begins to rise by the time they turn thirteen and above.

Importance of Teaching Empathy

Research reveals that empathy is something children learn throughout their childhood and teen years (Overgaauw et al., 2017). It has proven to be an essential life skill as it promotes the building of healthy and stable relationships. Young girls need it more because their interactions are varied. They have to deal with their parents, siblings, friends, and teachers. They are interacting with people of all ages all the time. Ask yourself this, if given the choice, would you have worked with someone inconsiderate, unkind, or hard-hearted? Or would you have preferred to work with someone kind, compassionate, and respectful towards your feelings, and emotions?

Another compelling reason to foster it in children, especially young girls because they get bullied, too. They are mocked for being fat, dark-skinned, or from a different race. Knowing what empathy is can put an end to bullying as every child is aware of how it feels to be in someone else's shoes. When they know how it feels like to be bullied, they are less likely to do it. They can place themselves in the situation the bullied is in, and comprehend how destructive it can be. Therefore, we believe that schools should focus more on building empathetic skills in kids than organizing redundant events all the time. However, for your daughter, it has to start at home.

Be Her Rock

For her to feel empathetic towards others, you have to fulfill her need for emotional support. If her own needs feel unfulfilled, she may not be able to show empathy towards others, she will be so consumed in her own set of problems that she would have no time to look at the problems of others and offer support.

Give Feelings a Name

Your teenage daughter is now at an age where she is introduced to several emotions and feelings. It can be hard for her to deal with them if she doesn't know how to identify them. For instance, many people, even adults, are unable to differentiate between frustration and anger. Giving feelings and emotions a name or label makes it easier to deal with it. Help her navigate through each negative emotion healthily.

Teach Her to Cope with Negative Emotions

Now that she is entering a new phase of her life, she is bound to get introduced to several new emotions such as anger, jealousy, rage, envy, melancholy, etc. Not knowing how to cope with them when she feels overwhelmed can lead to self-damaging habits. If she feels out of control or too much in pain over a breakup, she might try to deal with it in unhealthy ways. Each year, approximately 14.45% of young adults and adolescents try to end their lives by committing suicide. The rates are both shocking and alarming for parents. Therefore, from an early age, you must teach your children how to deal with emotions that make them feel out of control, in a positive and problem-solving way.

Ask Her How She Feels

Repeatedly asking her about her mental and emotional state can also prevent any attempts at suicide or self-harm early on. Kids are geared toward empathy naturally. Even if a toddler notices someone crying, they go up to them and hug them to make them feel better. However, as they grow older and become young adults, their focus becomes self-centered. They also start to hide stuff from their parents, which is why you have to keep probing questions about their mental and emotional state and keep a close eye on what they are up to. You can also role-play scenarios where you ask them how they would feel if someone did something bad to them and didn't show empathy.

Teach Her the Difference Between Good and Bad

Every day, we expose ourselves to several types of behaviors. Some are good, such as someone helping a homeless guy by buying them a meal from a restaurant. Some are bad, such as watching someone bully someone or making them sad. As a parent, you have to show her the difference between the two and talk about the effects each can have on someone. For instance, the homeless guy will be joyous whereas the guy who was bullied won't be.

Be a Good Role Model

Again, she is going to learn behaviors from you. If she notices that you are kind, considerate, and compassionate towards others, don't judge others and are always lending a helping hand, she will learn it, too. Show her how being charitable and selfless can be so rewarding. Show her what happiness and satisfaction it brings into your life.

Chapter 7: Essential Parenting Skill – Honesty

Teens and adults want the same thing from one another: transparency and honesty. They want to be able to say things to them without having to hide or manipulate it. They want open communication, empathetic support, and emotional comprehension from one another so that secrets and lies can be avoided. However, as your girl grows up to become a teenager, she starts to hide stuff from you, say lies to your face and act as if you are the one making a big deal of everything. Years of research have revealed that teens want to be honest with their parents only if they feel like they will be heard and not critiqued (Yau et al., 2009). They are more likely to be honest when they feel close to their parents and trust them to make decisions on their own. They expect parents to offer them some room to grow and not have to hide stuff.

On the other hand, another research, aimed to look at lying behaviors in different age groups ranging from 6 to 77, found that people are most dishonest when they are in the teen ages (Debey et al., 2015). So, what to believe and what not to?

Our suggestion, it doesn't matter. Your goal, as a parent, should be to raise honest children. Your goal should be to teach them about the importance of being transparent.

Lying is considered as one of the many developmental milestones that kids reach when they are about three years of age. Yes, it can be shocking to some but kids begin to lie by the time they turn three. As they grow older and comprehend the consequences and depth of it, they become less likely to lie unless they fear punishment, want to please others, to save face, get away with something or preserve others' feelings.

Everyone lies but it can be hurtful to be lied to. As a parent, you have to teach your girl about the dangers of it, so that she doesn't grow up to use lying as a means to get away with things or hide things from you. She needs to know that lying breaks trust, adds stress, compounds the problem but doesn't make it go away, ruins healthy relationships, and can always backfire.

How to Teach Her to Be More Honest?

As she grows up to become this amazing woman right before your eyes, you may want to be an active part of herself. However, you notice that she keeps to herself, only replies when questioned about something, and keeps secrets. For instance, you may find the light to her room open in the middle of the night and when you question her about it the next day, she says that she had fallen asleep way before that. It may get you curious as to why she is lying about it and not stating the truth. You may get suspicious and pry into her private space more. You may check her phone for messages to friends, read her Facebook chats, or go into her DMs on Instagram, all because of one small lie. You start to see her like some culprit and not trust anything she says. Do you see where this is going? It is turning you into a madwoman looking for some clue to prove her daughter wrong. Who will benefit from it, even if you prove her wrong?

All this inconvenience could have been avoided had she told you the truth in the first place, right?

So, what is the first thing you need to do here? Encourage her to be honest with you. How can you do that? By modeling honesty yourself. She shouldn't find you lying about being sick to skip work or lie to your partner about being late at work when you were celebrating the signing up of a new client at the bar with your colleagues. She doesn't need to see you making excuses to skip a family dinner on your partner's side because you have the flu or because you just don't want to go. Once she notices you taking the plunge for being late or going to dinners even when you don't feel like it, she will learn to do the same. She will learn to be accountable for her shortcomings and own up to her mistakes, even if she lands her in the pit. Other than that, you can:

Tell her How Hurtful Lying Can Be

She needs to know about the consequences of lying and how it can hurt people. She needs to get out of her little bubble and learn to care for others. To implant this wisdom in her, you have to sit her down and calmly discuss the dangers of being dishonest and why she shouldn't lie. Offer her your unconditional emotional support so that she knows she can turn to you with all of her problems instead of hiding them.

Reward Honesty

Rewarding or praising honesty is another way to nip the habit of lying in the bud. If she notices how happy it makes you when she tells the truth or how she doesn't get punished even when she comes up to you with information about something wrong that she did, she will start to do it more often. She will see it as a much easier way to deal with her problems because she knows that one lie can lead to another hundred and then another hundred to keep up with the previous ones.

Seek Reasons Behind Lying

Why is she lying to you? What could be the reason? What could she possibly be trying to hide? These are all questions you may want to ask yourself first and then her to know what's going on in her head that is compelling her to lie. Sometimes, teenagers lie when they are trying to protect someone or themselves from something inevitable. You must also know that kids don't lie out of habit; at least, not most of them do. They fear disappointing you and don't lie just for the sake of it either. Therefore, have a chat with her about why she feels the need to hide the truth and keep secrets and not come clean.

Don't Shame Her

If you notice that she has been frequently lying to you and others just to get away with things, talk to her instead of accusing or shaming her. Ask her about her fears and why she finds lying as her 'go-to' way to cope with things. Shaming her or accusing her when she gets caught red-handed will only make her sneakier with her lies and not address the issue.

Be a Good Listener

All children know the right thing to do but they just want to make things easier for themselves. Lying or cheating are things that allow us to get away with things in an easier manner. You have to allow her the freedom to choose for herself whilst ensuring her safety. You have to learn to listen and talk her through things in a compassionate manner so that she avoids taking the easy way out the next time. Keep in mind that you just have to guide them, not try to fix anything.

Chapter 8: Essential Parenting Skill – Responsibility

The teen years are the time when freedom looms large but family comes in between to prevent them from achieving that much-wanted independence. Parents want to raise their kids to become responsible adults whereas adolescents want to explore new things, go on adventures, and engage in risky behaviors and whatnot. Teaching kids to be accountable for their actions and grow up to become trustworthy and responsible adults is the job of every parent. To get started, they need to set some ground rules and guidelines that list their tasks, responsibilities, and commitments that are expected of them and also, age-appropriate. Of course, it isn't going to be an easy take and they may face resistance from their teenagers but they have to stand their ground.

Like most parents, you must dream of raising a responsible yet independent woman to one day. Someone that knows how to manage herself her emotions, friends, and family, follows her passions religiously and doesn't embarrass you or herself by falling short. No matter what, you have to continue to try in shaping her personality so that she is prepared to deal with the realities of adulthood.

Therefore, in this chapter, we look at how parents can teach their girls to become responsible adults, account for their behaviors and actions, and present themselves as civilized adults.

Teaching Her to Be Responsible

You may expect her to act like an adult but she is still too young to understand numerous things. After all, she is still growing and yet to face the many challenges life will throw at her as she enters another phase of her life: adulthood. Her social behavior is changing, thanks to the many hormonal changes inside her. She is confused, crying, yelling, running from chores, not owning up to her mistakes, and lying to you. What she needs is some guidance about accountability and responsibility. She needs to comprehend why some things must be done or owned up to even when she doesn't feel like it. It is your job to shape her behavior and you have to do it now. Below are some tips that will hopefully help you to raise her as a responsible adult.

Set Realistic Expectations

Start with setting some expectations for her to see if she complies or not. Don't leave her in the blind, thinking she will learn things through experience. When children know what is expected of them, they are more likely to live up to them. If the expectations are abstract or vague, they will avoid them. Setting realistic expectations is the first step in teaching her about responsibility. She must know what chores she has to do, why you expect her to clean her room and washroom, why she must dress modestly etc. she must also know what kind of behavior is expected of her, how she must remain disciplined and behave well.

Create a List of Chores

Doing chores is one of the most hateful things to a teen. No, she doesn't want to help you clean the fridge, wash the windows with soap and water or mop the floors. She wants you to do it. However, if she doesn't learn these things now, she will have a hard time adjusting to it when she leaves for college and gets a place of her own. Therefore, make a chores list and hang it on the fridge. Chores are an ideal way to teach about responsibility and the important role it plays in building discipline. She may resist doing them in the beginning but will eventually start to follow them out of habit soon. If she doesn't do them on purpose, let her know that there will be consequences.

Allow Her to Choose

Now that she is all growing up, make her see the importance of responsibility by allowing her to have a say in things concerning her and the family. For instance, if you are planning a trip for the summers, or planning to change houses, ask for her input on the matter. This will make her feel an important part of the family as well as give her a sense of responsibility. You can do the same with the chores. You can offer her a choice between doing the dishes and folding the laundry instead of asking her just one of the things. Whichever choice she picks, she is likely to get it done.

Have Consequences

If she deliberately avoids doing something and expects you to cover up for her, don't become a partner in it. She needs to learn about the consequences through experience. For example, she may want you to make up an excuse as to why she didn't finish her homework over the phone with her teacher. If she wasn't ill and purposely put it off, then don't be a part of the crime. Let her be punished. Let her be shamed in front of her classmates. She should know what punishment awaits her if she puts things off out of habit. Tell her that you reap what you sow.

Set Rewards for Achievements

If she does something good or something that was expected of her, reward her for it. It doesn't have to be a bribe or something tangible. It can be kind and appreciative words that boost her confidence and makes her more likely to repeat the same behaviors she got rewarded for. Besides, a little pat on the back or a little gift of appreciation doesn't require much work.

Engage Her in Volunteer Work

Volunteering broadens our minds and makes our souls delighted. It allows us to help others without expecting anything in return. For your daughter, it is a great way to see that the world has other people in it, too. It doesn't revolve around her only. When she will feel a part of an important cause, she will realize the privileges she has had and become responsible.

Set Goals with Her

If she has a passion or dream that she wants to follow, sit down, and draw out a roadmap together. Identify the steps she needs to take to reach her long-term goals. However, that is all you need to do and step back. The rest lies on her shoulders. Your job was only to help her navigate her options and paths. It is now her responsibility to make it happen. Sure, you can offer help if she asks for it but not before that!

Chapter 9: Essential Parenting Skill – Relationship Management

For most parents, navigating a teenager through adolescence is the most intimidating chapter of parenthood. They find them hard to discipline, set rules, and set expectations. They have trouble knowing when they can intervene in their lives and when they can't.

When it comes to relationships, things can be even harder because then you don't know how much they are sharing with you and keeping a secret, what activities are they involved in, are they being safe or not, etc. However, even a more thought-provoking question if they are practicing consensual sex or not. Sometimes, young girls are unaware of what touches and actions are appropriate. They end up complying with things they aren't ready for and give into abuse without even knowing that it accounts as such. Therefore, she needs to know the difference between a healthy and toxic relationship as well as the many types of abuses she may be subjected to, without proper knowledge.

A healthy relationship is one where respect, trust, communication, mutual understanding, and support prevails high. There must also be healthy boundaries between both partners and respected by them accordingly. An ideal partner mustn't want you to change and accept you for who you are. They should respect your personal choices and support you in your passions. The sex or any such activity leading to it must be consented upon by both partners before and none of them must feel obliged in some way to please the other.

Different Types of Abuses and Why She Should Know How to Distinguish Between Each

As stated earlier, she may be subjected to one or more of these abuses without knowledge. Therefore, as a parent, it is your job to introduce these to her and inquire if she feels like the relationship with her partner is abusive or not.

- Physical Abuse: This type of abuse occurs when one partner uses physical force to harm the other but the injuries incurred aren't visible to quality as such. This can include, kicking, choking, biting, and hitting, etc.
- Sexual Abuse: This type of abuse occurs when one partner tries to force themselves on to others without their consent or create surroundings where they feel helpless to save themselves from their partner. It can include restriction to use condoms or birth control, forced sexual activity, or pressuring the partner into doing something non-consensually.

- Emotional Abuse: This type of abuse occurs when one partner degrades, insults, manipulates, humiliates, or intimidates the other into doing things they don't want to do. They warn to leave them or tell lies about them if they don't agree with them.
- Digital Abuse: This is bullying your partner using technology. This can include taking pictures of them and making videos in a compromising situation and then using it to manipulate and blackmail them.

Teaching Her the Meaning of Healthy Relationships

Now that we have discussed the different types of abuses she may experience, she must know how to proceed with new relationships and approach sex when she feels ready for it. In this final section of the book, we discuss the many ways you can help her understand the different ideas, beliefs, and expectations regarding healthy relationships so that one day she can have one.

Talk Credibly

No need to skim through the conversation without going into the details. When giving her the talk, you have to answer all the questions she may have in her mind so that she stays safe and practices safe sex, too. If you aren't the talking kind, you can always send her links to websites that answer the questions well or send her to one of your friends or relatives she feels close to, to open up.

Set Boundaries and Expectations

Setting expectations and boundaries early on, such as expecting her to dress modestly when going or setting boundaries like, obliging to the time of the curfew, can help you both stay in your lanes. She will try not to break the rules and you won't have to spend all night worrying about whether she is safe or not. Some parents also put restrictions on who they can date and what qualities they should have to qualify to date her, but that is a far stretch.

Offer Support

She must, at all times, know that she can count on you for your support when she needs some help with her relationships. Lend her a compassionate ear and help her pick her options for birth control. You can also discuss the pros and cons of becoming a parent at an early age but not give her any idea that you are trying to intrude and decide for her.

Stay Neutral When Discussing Preferences

This heading wouldn't have made much sense had this book been written in the 80s or 90s but it matters now. When discussing with her about relationships and dating and how to involve in safe sex, don't assume that she must want to date a guy. You have to use gender-inclusive language and stay neutral without imposing a certain gender preference. If you do, she might think you won't understand or accept her if she chooses differently. This way, when you open up the possibility of her preferred sexual orientation, you will make it easier for them if they choose to come out of the closet someday and continue to find out where they fit in this world.

Be Respectful

Above all, show respect when talking to her about such things. You have to respect her individuality, beliefs, and opinions and come on to her in a non-obstructive or judging manner. This will open the line of healthy communication for you both and also get the job done.

Conclusion

Parenting isn't only about fulfilling the basic needs of our children. It is also about instilling good habits, imparting high values and morals, and preparing them for a life to be lived by them on their own. All of this is possible when we find a way to connect with them and keep the channels of communication open to cultivate strong relationships. With teenagers, this becomes a struggle because they start to have a mind of their own and view things differently. They are quick to judge and don't focus on the long-term aspects of things.

Your growing daughter may depict the same and want more privacy and independence. She may want to lead her life according to her rules. She may want to feel more in control of her decisions and preferences. She may no longer need you as a guide to problem-solve things for her.

But as any sane parent, you know what to do!

You know this isn't the time to sit back and watch her make a mess of her life. This is the time to be proactive and help them navigate their way towards success. This is the time to help her with her relationships. This is the time to teach her about compassion, responsibility, discipline, conflict management, and the need for transparency and good friends in her life so that she can lead a prosperous, confident, and successful life.

Thank you for giving this a read. I hope you loved it too because I certainly enjoyed writing it. It would make me the happiest if you would take a moment to leave an honest review. All you have to do is visit the site from where you purchased it. It's that simple! It doesn't have to be a full-fledged paragraph, just a few words will do too. Your few words will help others decide if this is what they should be reading too. Thank you in advance and best of luck with your parenting excursions. Surely, every moment is a joyous one with a kid.

References

Anderson, M. (2018). A Majority of Teens Have Experienced Some Form of Cyberbullying. In Pew Center Research (pp. 1–19). https://www.pewresearch.org/internet/wp-content/uploads/sites/9/2018/09/PI_2018.09.27_teens-and-cyberbullying_FINAL.pdf

Body image – tips for parents. (2012). Vic.Gov.Au. https://www.betterhealth.vic.gov.au/health/healthyliving/body-image-tips-for-parents

Chhandita Chakravarty. (2014, December 19). 10 Handy Tips On How To Make Your Teenager Responsible. MomJunction. https://www.momjunction.com/articles/handy-tips-make-teenager-responsible_00118480/

Debey, E., De Schryver, M., Logan, G. D., Suchotzki, K., & Verschuere, B. (2015). From junior to senior Pinocchio: A cross-sectional lifespan investigation of deception. Acta Psychologica, 160, 58–68. https://doi.org/10.1016/j.actpsy.2015.06.007

GoodTherapy.org. (2015, February 27). 9 Tips for Talking to Teens about Dating and Relationships. GoodTherapy.Org Therapy Blog. https://www.goodtherapy.org/blog/9-tips-for-talking-to-teens-about-dating-and-relationships-0227157

Graaff, J., Branje, S., Wied, M. D., Hawk, S., Lier, P. V., & Meeus, W. (2014). Perspective Taking and Empathic Concern in Adolescence: Gender Differences in Developmental Changes. Developmental Psychology, 50(3), 881–888. https://doi.org/https://doi.org/10.1037/a0034325

How to Help Teenagers Develop Empathy. (n.d.). www.melbournechildpsychology.com.au.https://www.melbournechildpsychology.com.au/blog/help-teenagers-develop-empathy/

Huebscher, B. (2010). Relationship Between Body Image and Self Esteem Among Adolescent Girls. In Search Results Web result with site links CiteSeerX (pp. 1–21). http://citeseerx.ist.psu.edu/viewdoc/download?doi=10.1.1.390.333&rep=rep1&type=pdf

Lee, K. (2019, June 29). How to Nurture Empathy and Emotional Intelligence in Children. Verywell Family. https://www.verywellfamily.com/how-to-nurture-empathy-in-kids-and-why-its-so-important-621098

Lindholm, M. (2018, May 10). 10 Rules for Living with a Teenage Daughter. Psychology Today. https://www.psychologytoday.com/intl/blog/more-women-s-work/201805/10-rules-living-teenage-daughter

Mabe, A. G., Forney, K. J., & Keel, P. K. (2014). Do you 'like' my photo? Facebook use maintains eating disorder risk. International Journal of Eating Disorders, 47(5), 516–523. https://doi.org/10.1002/eat.22254

Maciejewski, D. F., van Lier, P. A. C., Branje, S. J. T., Meeus, W. H. J., & Koot, H. M. (2015). A 5-Year Longitudinal Study on Mood Variability Across Adolescence Using Daily Diaries. Child Development, 86(6), 1908–1921. https://doi.org/10.1111/cdev.12420

Mann, T. (2018, May). Why do dieters regain weight? Https://Www.Apa.Org. https://www.apa.org/science/about/psa/201 8/05/calorie-deprivation

Miller, D. (2018, February 28). Enough. It's time to stop using the "mean girl" label for teenagers. Women's Agenda. https://womensagenda.com.au/leadership/a dvice/steps-help-teen-girls-resolve-conflict/

Overgaauw, S., Rieffe, C., Broekhof, E., Crone, E. A., & Güroğlu, B. (2017). Assessing Empathy across Childhood and Adolescence: Validation of the Empathy Questionnaire for Children and Adolescents (EmQue-CA). Frontiers in Psychology, 8. https://doi.org/10.3389/fpsyg.2017.00870

Rideout, V., & Robb, M. B. (2019). The Common Sense Census: Media Use by Tweens and Teens (J. Pritchett (Ed.)). Common Sense Media.

Saltz, G. (2016, February 16). How to Help Your Daughter Have a Healthy Body Image. Child Mind Institute; Child Mind Institute. https://childmind.org/article/how-to-help-your-daughter-have-a-healthy-body-image/

Yau, J. P., Tasopoulos-Chan, M., & Smetana, J. G. (2009). Disclosure to Parents About Everyday Activities Among American Adolescents From Mexican, Chinese, and European Backgrounds. Child Development, 80(5), 1481–1498. https://doi.org/10.1111/j.1467-8624.2009.01346.x

Young, K. (2016, June 1). When Children Lie – How to Respond and Build Honesty. www.heysigmund.com. https://www.heysigmund.com/when-children-lie/

Made in the USA
Coppell, TX
30 October 2022

85466601R00044